LABOUR AND DEVOLUTION IN WALES

LABOUR AND DEVOLUTION IN WALES

JOHN GILBERT EVANS

First impression: 2019
© John Gilbert Evans & Y Lolfa Cyf., 2019

Cover design: Y Lolfa
Cover picture: Alamy

ISBN: 978 1 78461 803 2

Published and printed in Wales
on paper from well-maintained forests by
Y Lolfa Cyf., Talybont, Ceredigion SY24 5HE
e-mail ylolfa@ylolfa.com
website www.ylolfa.com
tel 01970 832 304
fax 832 782

Preface

IN WALES, THE predominance of the Labour Party at parliamentary and local government levels has meant that any study of devolution is largely devoted to the approach adopted by Labour. Initially, after the rejection of the Labour government's devolution proposals in a referendum in 1979, the Labour Party in Wales was reluctant to embrace the issue. However, by the mid 1980s it had come round to supporting an assembly and this was endorsed by the party centrally in the late 1980s. Eventually, after extensive debate and consultation, the party managed to reconcile its differences and succeeded in framing a policy that gained the support, but only just, of the electorate in Wales in a referendum in 1997. Consequently, the Government of Wales Act 1998 established a National Assembly for Wales.

I am indebted to several people for the ready assistance which they gave me in preparing this study. I wish to express my gratitude to Professor Ralph A. Griffiths, Swansea, for his advice and support, and to Professor Chris Williams,

University College, Cork, for invaluable comments which enhanced the work. The drafts were reproduced by Rhodri W. Evans and his efforts are very much appreciated. I also wish to record my thanks to Lefi Gruffudd and staff at Y Lolfa for their cooperation and assistance.

John Gilbert Evans
Penarth
2019

Contents

Contents

PART I

Background (1886–1979)

THE QUESTION OF Home Rule for Ireland which occupied W.E. Gladstone and the Liberals at the end of the 19th century had consequences in Wales. *Cymru Fydd* (Young Wales) was founded in 1886 with the aim of persuading the Liberal Party to grant Wales a legislative assembly and greater recognition. Gladstone's government had earlier passed the Welsh Sunday Closing Act in 1881 prohibiting public houses from opening on Sundays. However, it was a Conservative government supported by Liberal Unionists that passed the Intermediate Education Act of 1889, which resulted in the establishment of a system of secondary education, but it was a Liberal government that granted a charter to the University of Wales in 1893. In 1891 and 1892 when *Cymru Fydd* was a dominant force, bills to appoint a secretary of state were introduced, but only received a first reading. Welsh Liberalism though did not embrace *Cymru Fydd*. In 1895 the North Wales Liberal Federation agreed to join with the movement, but in 1896 the proposal was rejected by the South Wales Liberal Association. This was the movement's death knell. After the House of Lords had defeated Gladstone's Home Rule Bill for Ireland which had been forced through the House of Commons, the Liberals were defeated at the polls by the Conservatives in 1895. Following the demise of *Cymru Fydd* enthusiasm for changes in the machinery of government waned, but later, in 1907, the Liberals granted charters to the National Museum of Wales and the National Library of Wales and in the same year the Welsh Department of the Board of Education was founded. A bill was introduced in 1914 for the appointment of a secretary of state, but it received little support.[1]

During the First World War and for a few years after its end Welsh industries flourished and rural Wales benefited too. The prosperity came to an end in 1923 and a period of 'almost unrelieved depression' followed that lasted up to the beginning of the Second World War.[2] The consequences of the Depression were evident in all parts of the United Kingdom, but south Wales was one of the most severely affected areas. Employment in south Wales was dependant on heavy industries and particularly on the production and export of coal. The decline of this export trade and the export of other raw materials had dire consequences in the area.[3] There was an extremely high level of unemployment. An industrial survey revealed that in December 1930 the rate in industrial south Wales was 31.8 per cent and earlier, in January, 87,854 people had been granted poor relief.[4] It also showed that this high level of unemployment had led to mass migration from the area. Monmouthshire was badly affected. The losses in Blaina/

Nantyglo and Abertillery were 28.6 per cent and 29.4 per cent respectively.[5] In 1934, the area coterminous with the south Wales coalfield was designated a special area by the Ministry of Labour.[6] In that year unemployment in the eastern area of the coalfield beyond Port Talbot was 44.5 per cent, far higher than it was in the western area where it was 28.6 per cent.[7] Despite a population decrease because of migration between 1931 and 1935, unemployment was still high in 1935 at 39.1 per cent and 39.5 per cent in 1936.[8] During this difficult economic period bills were introduced to secure a secretary of state or 'to provide for the better government of Wales...' Interestingly one bill in 1922 was 'to provide for the better government of Scotland and Wales...'[9] The bills, as expected, made little progress. Coupling Wales with Scotland was a tactic that would be used by Labour governments in the 1970s and 1990s.

In the 1920s there were other developments on the political front. In 1925 a Welsh Nationalist Party was formed, but in spite of the circumstances prevailing it made little impact. Another was the emergence of the Labour Party as a political force. In the 1922 general election Labour's representation increased to 18 and it replaced the Liberals as Wales's major political party. The number increased to 19 in 1923, but dropped to 16 in 1924. In 1929, 25 seats were held by Labour and in 1931 when the number fell to 15, four of its MPs in south Wales were returned unopposed and that number became 10 in 1935 when the party held 18 seats.[10] Several of these MPs were former miners and former students of the Central Labour College and its teaching based on Marx's economic and political theory was to determine the approach of some to devolution.[11]

In the 1930s and 1940s there were renewed demands for a secretary of state. A bill for a secretary of state presented in 1937 was again unsuccessful.[12] There were demands too from individual MPs and from the Welsh Parliamentary Party comprising of all Welsh MPs. A delegation from the party met the prime minister Neville Chamberlain in 1938, but like every other attempt the request was turned down.[13] During the War a Welsh Day was conceded by the coalition government and the first debate in the House of Commons on Welsh affairs was held on 17 October 1944.[14] There was support too for a secretary of state within the Labour movement in Wales. The South Wales Regional Council of Labour consisting of constituency and trade union representatives supported such an appointment at its conferences in 1942, 1943 and 1944.[15] James Griffiths (Labour, Llanelli) was a keen advocate at this time.[16] The appointment was also supported by Welsh local authorities, and at a conference in 1943 their association passed a resolution urging the government 'to proceed immediately with the appointment of a Secretary of State for Wales and

Monmouthshire'.[17] In north Wales too there was support from Labour parliamentary candidates prior to the 1945 election, but it was made clear that such an appointment had not been approved by the party centrally.[18] That was to be a stumbling block in future years.

Following its election victory in 1945 Labour in government, not unexpectantly, had little sympathy for the appointment of a secretary of state.[19] It thought that measures that related to the United Kingdom would be more beneficial to Wales than changes in government administration. Even a minister for Welsh affairs without departmental responsibilities, as proposed in a memorandum by Ness Edwards (Labour, Caerphilly) in 1946, was rejected.[20] Surprisingly, Edwards made the point that such an appointment would recognize Wales as a nation, but that plea too fell on deaf ears.[21] In 1947 the South Wales Regional Council of Labour had merged with the North Wales Federation of Labour Parties to form the Welsh Regional Council of Labour. This new body recognized now that the appointment of a secretary of state 'could not be fruitfully pursued', and in 1948 at a conference with the Welsh Parliamentary Labour Party an advisory council was supported.[22] This proposal had already been endorsed by the Welsh Parliamentary Labour Party, and in November 1948 the government announced the establishment of an advisory council, viz. the Council for Wales and Monmouthshire.[23] Subsequently, the demand for a secretary of state fell away and a bill in 1949 to provide for an appointment was again unsuccessful.[24]

Following its election victory in 1951, the Conservative government kept the party's pledge to appoint a minister for Welsh affairs and the home secretary David Maxwell-Fyfe was given the responsibility.[25] The appointment, although it gave Wales greater recognition, was derided by Labour MPs and the party did not think it worthwhile to appoint a shadow minister for Welsh affairs.[26] The motive behind the Conservative decision to make the appointment is unclear. Electorally, a few seats were gained by the Conservatives. They had gained one seat in 1950, bringing the party's representation to three and that figure became five in 1951 and 1955 when they held more seats than the Liberals.[27]

In the early 1950s the Welsh Question was a real problem for the Labour Party. It all began when *Undeb Cymru Fydd* (New Wales Union), a voluntary non-political organization, called a conference in 1950 to consider home rule for Wales.[28] The Welsh Regional Council of Labour immediately disassociated the party from the conference.[29] At the conference a committee was elected, and it was decided in 1951 to organize a petition to parliament supporting a legislative parliament.[30] Against the party's diktat, five Labour MPs, S.O. Davies (Merthyr Tydfil), Cledwyn Hughes (Anglesey), T.W. Jones (Meirioneth), Goronwy Roberts (Caernarvonshire) and Tudor Watkins (Brecon and Radnor) actively supported the Parliament for Wales Campaign. Being at odds with the party made life difficult for these MPs.[31] Eventually Labour was forced to respond, and in its policy statement *Labour's Policy for Wales* in 1954 there was a commitment to appoint a minister for Welsh affairs with a seat in the cabinet and to the revision of the constitution of the Council for Wales and Monmouthshire, to make it a more effective and representative body.[32] Immediately afterwards, S.O. Davies presented a private member's bill 'to provide for the better government of Wales...'[33] The bill was given a second reading in March 1955, but at the close of the debate it was as expected defeated.[34] The following year, Goronwy Roberts on behalf of the Parliament for Wales Campaign, presented a petition to the House of Commons. It only had 240,652 signatures which was a disappointment to its organizers.[35]

The Parliament for Wales Campaign had not succeeded in getting any tangible results, but an important development was imminent. In 1957, the Council for Wales and Monmouthshire published its *Third Memorandum* on central government administration in Wales. In it, the Council's main recommendation was that a secretary of state be appointed with a seat in the cabinet and a Welsh Office established.[36] After the memorandum was presented to the government, prime minister Harold Macmillan, like his Conservative predecessors, rejected the recommendation.[37]

The Welsh Parliamentary Labour Party had accepted the recommendation in the memorandum, but the Welsh Regional Council of Labour's executive committee had not.[38] James Griffiths supported the recommendation when Labour's tripartite committee, consisting of representatives of the National Executive Committee, the Welsh Parliamentary Labour Party and the Welsh Regional Council of Labour met in 1959 to consider a policy for Wales.[39] Ness Edwards disagreed with Griffiths and the committee agreed to recommend a minister without a department.[40] However, Hugh Gaitskell intervened and after he had consulted the Welsh Parliamentary Labour Party, the recommendation to the National Executive Committee was that a secretary of state with responsibilities be appointed.[41] Although the Welsh Regional Council of Labour disagreed with the decision, the National Executive Committee gave its approval.[42] As leader and deputy leader, Gaitskell and Griffiths worked closely together and that obviously was a factor when the decision was taken. Goronwy Roberts had proposed a Welsh Grand Committee in 1953 and in 1956, and in

1958 Ness Edwards, who had always been interested in the machinery of government, submitted a memorandum to the Select Committee on Procedure and a Welsh Grand Committee was established in 1960.[43]

Labour's triumph, led by Harold Wilson in the 1964 general election, resulted in the appointment of a secretary of state and the creation of the Welsh Office. James Griffiths, appropriately, was the first incumbent, and was given responsibility for roads and nearly all the executive functions of the Housing and Local Government Office in Wales.[44] Each subsequent secretary of state sought extra functions, thus creating a sizeable government department. The Welsh Office has also sponsored legislation, sometimes in conjunction with other departments. Almost immediately after its re-election in 1966 the government faced a series of crises in quick succession. Then it lost a by-election in Carmarthen to Gwynfor Evans, president of Plaid Cymru (Welsh Nationalist Party).[45] Cledwyn Hughes, who had succeeded James Griffiths as secretary of state, hoped to establish an all Wales elected council, but his proposals were rejected by the Cabinet in 1967.[46] Apparently, there was opposition too from Welsh Labour MPs.[47] In its place, the government intended to replace the Welsh Economic Council set up in 1965 with an 'advisory and promotional body', the Welsh Council.[48] Following the loss of the by-election in Carmarthen, there were further shocks for

Labour. They were to come very close to losing what were rock-solid Labour seats to Plaid Cymru, Rhondda West in 1967 and Caerphilly in 1968.[49] During the same period, bills to establish a parliament for Wales, federal parliaments for Scotland and Wales and Northern Ireland, and a bill 'to authorize referenda in Scotland and Wales' were introduced. Again, they made little progress.[50] The upsurge in support for the nationalists in its heartlands rattled the Labour Party and it faced a real dilemma. Was the support likely to grow or was it only a protest vote against the government? In order to avoid a hasty decision which it might regret, the government decided that the answer was to appoint a royal commission on the constitution.[51] Emrys Jones, who had been appointed party organizer in Wales in 1965, persuaded the party to appoint a study group to prepare evidence for submission to the royal commission.[52] The evidence presented fell short of what the group had proposed.[53] In January 1970, the Labour Party in Wales advocated an elected council with 'its roots in local government'. This council could also undertake the work of nominated bodies and central government functions which could be 'undertaken at a Welsh level'.[54] In the previous December, the Welsh Parliamentary Labour Party had made its views known to the National Executive Committee. It opposed the transfer of ministerial functions to a council which could be established to exercise democratic control of nominated bodies. It was emphasized that Labour councillors would oppose the transfer to the council of local government functions.[55] Labour, in its manifesto for the 1970 general election, promised to establish an elected council with 'extended powers'.[56] The election was won by the Conservative Party led by Edward Heath. In May 1973, the Welsh Parliamentary Labour Party restated its support for an elected council and in November 1973, after the publication of the royal commission's report, it supported an assembly to exercise 'closer democratic control over the distinctive features of Welsh life'.[57]

In the general election in February 1974, Labour's Welsh manifesto promised an elected council 'to be an effective democratic force in the life of Wales', but there was no mention of devolution in the national manifesto.[58] In the election, the nationalists in Scotland and Wales gained four seats from Labour and four from the Conservatives.[59] They were perceived now to be a real threat and the newly-elected minority Labour government led by Wilson responded at once, although some cabinet members were not convinced of the need to do so.[60] John Morris (Aberavon), a committed devolutionist, was appointed secretary of state and not the shadow secretary of state, George Thomas (Cardiff, West), who was hostile to devolution. In the October general election, the government in the national manifesto promised an assembly and not an elected council as was promised in February in its Welsh manifesto.[61] That immediately sent alarm bells ringing. In the election Labour was returned, but only with a three-seat majority.[62] In 1975 the anxieties of the Welsh Parliamentary Labour Party were conveyed to the government and to the executive of the Labour Party in Wales. The MPs confirmed the decision taken in 1973.[63] Thereafter, the government's proposals were opposed by a number of MPs led by Neil Kinnock and Leo Abse, both representing Gwent constituencies. The proposals were also opposed by some party members in Wales who supported a legislative assembly.

Immediately after the February election there had been a demand for a referendum which was rejected in June 1974 by the Labour Party in Wales.[64] In January 1976, local authorities declared their support for a referendum and the demand received a boost when the *Western Mail* in March stated, 'We now believe, in short, that there should be a referendum.'[65] By December 1976, 151 MPs had signed Leo Abse's amendment calling for a referendum and the government relented and announced that the proposals for Scotland and Wales would be the subject of referenda before the act took effect.[66] After their success, opponents of the bill then proceeded to demand that the proposals for Scotland and Wales be included in separate bills. It was apparent that the Scottish proposals because of the

Scottish National Party threat were of greater importance to the government. It would also be easier to have the Welsh proposals passed if they were accommodated in a joint bill.[67] Yet another concession followed when separate bills were agreed in July 1977.[68] When the Wales Bill was being debated in April 1978, opponents called for the inclusion of a threshold requirement of 40 per cent of the eligible electorate to be in favour, and the government again obliged by moving an amendment to that effect and a clause was duly inserted.[69] Welsh MPs opposed to the bills were supported by their counterparts in England. Early in the debates members representing English constituencies feared that Scotland and Wales would gain at the expense of the English regions.[70] Those MPs were supported by economic planning councils and local authorities in their regions.[71]

During debates the objections to the proposals were continually expounded. It was claimed that they would inevitably lead to the break-up of the United Kingdom, that the number of MPs representing Wales would be reduced and that the office of secretary of state could be abolished.[72] Other issues were raised that probably struck a chord with the electorate later. The cost of setting up and running an assembly was highlighted, and Leo Abse who represented an anglicized area made the Welsh language an issue, claiming that English speakers with no knowledge of Welsh would be governed by 'a Welsh-speaking bureaucratic elite'.[73] Local authorities since the 1960s had been part of the devolution debate, and had always objected to the loss of functions to an all Wales elected body and to further reorganization.[74] Therefore, inserting a clause in the bill granting the assembly powers to review local government was an error of judgement on the government's part.[75]

The Wales Bill was introduced in November 1977 and received the royal assent on 31 July 1978. In the referendum that followed on 1 March 1979 the proposals were overwhelmingly rejected. Only 243,048 declared their support for the measure, but 956,330 opposed it. There were a number of reasons for the Act's rejection, apart from the arguments advanced during the referendum campaign. The referendum was held in March and during a period of industrial action by local government employees, and the effects were certainly felt by the electorate.[76] North Wales had fears that an assembly would be dominated by representatives from south Wales and in south Wales the language issue may also have played a part.[77] The press as expected played its part. The London dailies, read by the majority in Wales, gave the issue scant attention and in Wales, press opinion was divided.[78] Although they were Labour Party proposals supported by the Wales Trade Union Council, they were not supported by party and trade union members.[79] Also, by 1979 the debate had gone on for too long, and the issue was of little significance during what was to be termed the 'winter of discontent'.

After the loss of a vote of confidence James Callaghan, who had succeeded Wilson as prime minister in 1976, resigned and the Conservatives led by Margaret Thatcher won the election in May. The newly-elected Conservative government kept the commitment that a select committee on Welsh affairs be appointed and it was approved by the House of Commons in June 1979.[80]

References

1   David Williams, *A History of Modern Wales* (London,1950), 279–81, 283. John Davies, *A History of Wales* (London, 1993), 446, 454, 466. G.M. Trevelyan, *History of England* (London, 1945), 688–89. House of Commons Library, Parliamentary Information List, *Bills on devolution in Wales*, SN/PC/04753, 12 June 2008.

2   Williams, *A History of Modern Wales*, 287.

3   Board of Education, *Educational Problems of the South Wales Coalfield*, 1931 (Educational Pamphlets No. 88), 5–7.

4   Board of Trade, *An Industrial Survey of South Wales*, 1932, 10, 174.

5   *Idem.*, 6, 165.

6   Ministry of Labour, *Reports of Investigations into the Industrial Conditions in certain Depressed Areas*, 1934 (Cmd. 4728), 128.

7   *Idem.*, 129–30.

8   *First Report of the Commissioner for the Special Areas (England and Wales)*, 1935 (Cmd. 4957), 94, 98. *Report of the Commissioner for the Special Areas in England and Wales for the year ended 30 September 1937*, 1937 (Cmd. 5595), 19. *Third Report of the Commissioner for the Special Areas (England and Wales)*, 1936 (Cmd. 5303), 175.

9   House of Commons Library, Parliamentary Information List, *op. cit.*

10 Beti Jones, *Parliamentary Elections in Wales, 1900–75* (Talybont, 1977), 59, 78, 85–9, 91–5.

11 W.W. Craik, *The Central Labour College 1909–29* (London, 1964), 117, 124, 173–6, 184.

12 House of Commons Library, Parliamentary Information List, *op. cit.*

13 James Griffiths, *Pages from Memory* (London, 1969), 158–9.

14 The National Archives, CAB. 65 41, WM (44) 27, 3 March 1944. *Parl. Deb.*, vol. 403, cols. 2240–98, 2315.

15 *Report of the Annual Conference of South Wales Regional Council of Labour*, 16 May 1942, 6, 15. *Ibid.*, 15 May 1943, 16. *Ibid.*, 6 May 1944, 16.

16 *Y Cymro*, 25 April 1942.

17 University of Swansea, S.O. Davies Papers, B1, Association of Welsh Local Authorities, Memorandum to the Welsh Parliamentary Party, March 1944.

18 *Y Cymro*, 16 February 1945. Labour Party Archives, M. Phillips Papers, M. Phillips to Labour Party worker in Bangor, 15 June 1945.

19 The National Archives, CAB. 128/5, CM (46) 9, 28 January 1946.

20 *Ibid.*, PREM, 8 1569 Part 1, MG (46) 7, 17 May 1946.

21 *Ibid.*, MG (46) 2, 17 July 1946.

22 Welsh Regional Council of Labour, *Annual Meeting*, 17 April 1948, 6. *Western Mail*, 21 June 1948.

23 *Western Mail*, 28 May 1948. *Parl. Deb.*, vol. 458, cols. 1262–77.

24 House of Commons, Parliamentary Information List, *op. cit.*

25 *Parl. Deb.*, vol. 493, col. 75.

26 University of Swansea, S.O. Davies Papers A2, S.O. Davies to Carol Johnson, Secretary, Parliamentary Labour Party, 16 February 1956.

27 Jones, *Parliamentary Elections*, 106, 113, 119.

28 Parliament for Wales Campaign, *Parliament for Wales* (Aberystwyth, 1953), 3.

29 Welsh Regional Council of Labour, *Annual Meeting*, 13 May 1950, 11.

30 *Parliament for Wales*, 3, 7–8.

31 Labour Party Archives, M. Phillips Papers, C. Prothero to M. Phillips, 6 October 1953. Welsh Regional Council of Labour, *Annual Meeting*, 26 May 1956, 13.

32 Labour Party, *Labour's Policy for Wales* (Cardiff, 1954), 11–12.

33   House of Commons, Parliamentary Information List, *op. cit.*

34   *Parl. Deb.*, vol. 537, cols. 2526–8.

35   *Ibid.*, vol. 551, col. 1589.

36   The Council for Wales and Monmouthshire, *Third Memorandum by the Council on its Activities*, January 1957 (Cmnd. 53), 50–1, 80, 84–5.

37   *Government Administration in Wales, Text of a letter addressed by the Prime Minister to the Chairman of the Council for Wales and Monmouthshire*, 11 December 1957 (Cmnd. 334), 4–5.

38   Labour Party, *Annual Report 1957*, 67. Labour Party Archives, M. Phillips Papers, C. Prothero to M. Phillips, 17 September 1957.

39   Labour Party Archives, Tripartite Committee on Welsh Policy Statement, report of first meeting, 16 April 1959, 1–6.

40   *Ibid.*, draft for consideration by Home Policy Committee, Re. 576/June 1959, 20.

41   *Ibid.*, minutes of fifth meeting, 21 July 1959.

42   The Labour Party National Executive Committee, minutes, 22 July 1959.

43   *Parl. Deb.*, vol. 510, cols. 485–6. *Ibid.*, vol. 548, cols. 680–2. Minutes of evidence taken before the Select Committee on Procedure, 15 July 1958, 131–6. Standing Orders, 61–2.

44   *Parl. Deb.*, vol. 702, cols. 623–4, 626–7.

45   *Western Mail*, 16 July 1966.

46   Lord Cledwyn, *The Referendum: The End of an Era* (Cardiff, 1981), 12.

47   *Western Mail*, 30 June 1967.

48   *Local Government in Wales*, July 1967 (Cmnd. 3340), 21–2.

49   Jones, *Parliamentary Elections*, 147.

50   House of Commons Library, Parliamentary Information List, *op. cit.*

51   *Parl. Deb.*, vol. 772, col. 9.

52 Welsh Council of Labour, *Report to the Annual Meeting*, 15–16 May 1970, 6.

53 David Foulkes, J. Barry Jones, R.A. Wilford (eds.), *The Welsh Veto: The Wales Act 1978 and the Referendum* (Cardiff, 1983), 23.

54 *Evidence of the Labour Party in Wales to the Commission on the Constitution*, 7 January 1970, 12. Commission on the Constitution, *Minutes of Evidence 5: Wales*, 1972, 23, 26.

55 Labour Party Archives, Memorandum on devolution in Wales presented to the National Executive Committee by the Welsh Group of Labour MPs, 1969.

56 Labour Party, *Now Britain's strong let's make it great to live in* (London, 1970), 21.

57 University of Swansea, Fred Evans Papers, A8, statement recommending an elected assembly for Wales, 1973, 1–2. *Western Mail*, 7 November 1973.

58 Labour Party, *Labour's Policies for a Brighter Future for Wales* (Cardiff, February 1974). *Ibid.*, *Let us work together. Labour's way out of the crisis*, (February 1974).

59 David Butler and Dennis Kavanagh, *The British General Election of February 1974* (London and Basingstoke, 1974), 260.

60 Barbara Castle, *The Castle Diaries 1974–76* (London, 1980), 173.

61 Labour Party, *Labour Party Manifesto*, October 1974, 21.

62 David Butler and Dennis Kavanagh, *The British General Election of 1979* (London and Basingstoke, 1980), 18.

63 *Western Mail*, 26 February 1975. *Welsh Council of Labour, Report to the Annual Meeting*, 14–15 May 1976, 16.

64 *Welsh Council of Labour, Report to the Annual Meeting,* 9–10 May 1975, 37.

65 *Parl. Deb.*, vol. 903, col. 902. *Western Mail*, 28 November 1975. *Ibid.*, 17 January 1976. *Ibid.*, 19 March 1976.

66 *Parl. Deb.*, vol. 922, cols. 1725–7, 1736–7, 1794.

67   *Ibid.*, vol. 924, col. 113.

68   *Ibid.*, vol. 936, col. 313.

69   *Ibid.*, vol. 948, col. 457.

70   *Ibid.*, vol. 885, cols. 1195, 1197.

71   Northern Economic Planning Council, views on *Our Changing Democracy: Devolution to Scotland and Wales* (Cmnd. 6348), 28 January 1976, 2. Tyne and Wear County Council, *Devolution: The Case Against. Is this a United Kingdom?*, a document produced following a seminar on 7 January 1977, 2, 4.

72   *Parl. Deb.*, vol. 885, cols. 1032, 1059. *Ibid.*, vol. 903, cols. 300, 599–600, 683, 706.

73   *Ibid.*, vol. 903, col. 686. *Ibid.*, vol. 918, col. 1753.

74   Commission on the Constitution, *Written Evidence 7: Wales* (1972), 68, 2, 5.

75   Association of County Councils, Executive Council Minutes, February 1978, 323.

76   Butler and Kavanagh, *The British General Election of 1979*, 24.

77   Kenneth O. Morgan, *Rebirth of a Nation: Wales 1880–1980* (Oxford, 1981), 405. The Labour Party, news release, 21 February 1979, 6.

78   Foulkes, Jones and Wilford (eds.), *Welsh Veto*, 154–62, 169, 171, 177, 192.

79   Private Information.

80   Conservative Party, *Putting Britain First: A National Policy from the Conservatives* (London, October, 1974), 27. *Ibid.*, *Conservative Manifesto for Wales* (1979). *Parl. Deb.*, vol. 969, cols. 359–61.

PART II

Labour's Continuing Debate
(1983–1997)

THE SHEER SCALE of the rejection of an assembly in the referendum in 1979 suggested that devolution would not be a major issue in Welsh politics in the foreseeable future. The only party that could possibly deliver an assembly was the Labour Party, but after such a veto the Labour Party in Wales was reluctant to revisit the subject.[1] In contrast, in England the need to decentralize government administration to regional authorities was raised by Labour politicians. In January 1983, John Prescott, Opposition spokesman on regional affairs and devolution, speaking at a Labour Party in Wales conference, emphasized a need for greater accountability in government administration.[2] Shortly afterwards in March, the Labour Party's National Executive Committee declared that the party, when next in government, would establish an assembly with tax raising powers in Scotland and planning boards in Wales and the regions of England, in conjunction with the restructuring of local government.[3]

From the outset, Scotland was to be treated differently from Wales and the English regions. Labour suffered a heavy defeat in the general election in June 1983 and Neil Kinnock succeeded Michael Foot as party leader in October. In 1985, the question of regional administration in England was raised by Jack Straw, Labour's spokesman on the environment. He pointed out that there was a system of regional administration of central government functions, and the issue therefore was whether or not there was a need for it to be 'democratically controlled'.[4]

The mood within the Labour Party in Wales was changing and it had set up a working party to re-examine the machinery of government. In March 1986, its executive accepted the working party's recommendation that an elected assembly be established together with a single tier local government structure. The assembly would take over the work of nominated bodies and would also have some responsibilities in the economic field. Crucially, the changes were to be implemented in Wales along with similar changes in the English regions. However, for the executive the priority in Wales was the creation of employment opportunities.[5] In May, it was recommended that in the short term a Welsh economic council be established, chaired by the secretary of state and comprising of representatives of local government and other public bodies.[6] Such a council would hopefully enhance Wales's economic prospects.

The democratic deficit at local level was still an issue in England. In August, David Blunkett, Labour leader of Sheffield City Council and a member of Labour's local government committee, reiterated the view that there was a lack of democratic accountability at regional level.[7] *The*

Daily Express, in a leading article, was quite forthright in its opposition to any changes. It thought that the Labour Party's proposals for regional government coupled with the local government changes envisaged were 'misconceived', and the reform of the latter would be 'as dreadful as the last shake-up, perpetuated in 1972 by the Heath Government'.[8] Although the Labour Party in Wales's executive had the previous year supported an assembly, the Labour Party in its 1987 general election manifesto, *Britain Will Win*, repeated the policy agreed by the National Executive Committee in 1983 and only promised an economic planning council for Wales. In addition it pledged to consult widely on the 'most effective regional structure of government and administration in England and Wales'.[9] The need to consult suggested that any changes would not be imminent and they would not necessarily be similar in both countries. Rather surprisingly, after Labour's general election defeat in June, the issue of regional and local government was immediately back on its agenda. Again, it emphasized that any changes would be introduced in both England and Wales simultaneously, which would dispel the charge that the policy was nationalistic.[10] The Labour Party in Wales again supported an assembly to be established as part of local government reform.[11]

In May 1988, the Labour Party in Wales conference approved a consultative document on local government reform which proposed four options, and two of them included the creation of an assembly to be responsible for Welsh Office functions. A final decision would be taken after a twelve-month period of consultation.[12] However, Alan Williams (Swansea West), Opposition spokesman on Welsh affairs, had reservations regarding an assembly. In his view, its work and finances would not be free from the restrictions of Westminster governments.[13] Neil Kinnock, who had opposed the Labour government's proposals in the 1970s, recognized that there had been an increase in the centralization of government and that some functions could be administered at local level, but others would be better administered on a 'county or subregional or regional basis with democratic accountability'. Although, he said, the aim should be to 'stop the Thatcherite dictation from the centre and the cuts that come with it'.[14] He later made it clear that he was not in favour of institutions which would result in the reduction in the number of MPs at Westminster from different parts of the United Kingdom. But he thought that more accountable and efficient government was required to meet people's needs.[15]

Meanwhile, a cross-party organization had been set up to gain support for the devolution of central government functions. In November 1988, the Campaign for a Welsh Assembly held its inaugural conference in Merthyr Tydfil. Devolution was certainly not a burning issue in Wales, but

Denzil Davies (Labour, Llanelli) claimed that there was an increase in support for it because of the policies of the Thatcher governments. He thought that a Welsh assembly 'would be a counterweight to the increasing centralisation of government'.[16] The Conservative government was certainly not contemplating changes to the machinery of government, and the view expressed by Nicholas Bennett (Conservative, Pembroke) in an article by John Osmond that an assembly would simply result in another layer of government was reminiscent of the 1970s debate.[17]

In the month prior to the Pontypridd by-election in 1989, devolution of government was an issue, perhaps because of the possible threat from Plaid Cymru. Plaid Cymru had come close to defeating Labour in two by-elections in south-east Wales in the 1960s. There had been another close call in 1972. In the Merthyr Tydfil by-election Plaid Cymru had come second to Labour, and Ted Rowlands, the Labour candidate's majority was less than expected at 3,710. Roy Hattersley, Labour's deputy leader, speaking in Bristol, promised that Labour in government would establish regional assemblies in the United Kingdom with powers to legislate and raise revenue.[18] Although, as the *Western Mail* stated in its editorial, there was no evidence that voters supported devolution. Hattersley claimed at a meeting in Pontypridd, as had Denzil Davies before him, that the case was 'overwhelming' because of the 'excesses' of the

Thatcher governments. Hattersley repeated his promise that assemblies for Scotland, Wales and the regions of England would be established, but the specific functions to be exercised were not stipulated.[19] Neil Kinnock was not as explicit. He supported devolution, but in his view different structures would be needed in different parts of the United Kingdom, and the concept should be offered as 'having merit in itself and not simply responding to centralisation undertaken by one government'.[20] He then raised the possibility of Wales having 'two or three assemblies to meet the special regional interests of the country'.[21] Kim Howells, Labour's candidate in the Pontypridd by-election, disagreed with that assertion, saying, 'Wales is a nation and should have its own assembly'.[22]

The Labour Party made its position clear in May 1989, when its National Executive Committee agreed that an incoming Labour government would devolve powers to assemblies in Scotland, Wales and the regions of England. This decision enabled the Labour Party in Wales to begin framing a detailed policy.[23] In Wales, as time went on, the effects of the Thatcher government's policies did help to convince Labour activists in particular that devolution should be supported. Speaking at the Labour Party in Wales conference, Derek Gregory, secretary in Wales of the National Union of Public Employees, declared that devolution was a means of escape from 'the yoke of

Thatcher and the Treasury'.[24] That was an overstatement because the Westminster government was responsible for United Kingdom economic policies, and the Treasury would determine the block grant allocated to an assembly. While the effects of Margaret Thatcher's policies had helped to reignite a demand for devolution within the Labour Party in Wales, she was not prepared to engage in any discussion of the issue. She merely reminded MPs that the last Labour government's devolution policy had been rejected by a huge majority in a referendum.[25] One of her MPs though, Jonathan Evans (Brecon and Radnor), thought that another referendum was apposite and suggested that it be supported by all parties.[26] He was to repeat the request for a referendum on several occasions later.

The Labour Party in Wales annual conference in 1989 had considered the four options presented to it by a working party and accepted one that proposed the creation of an assembly.[27] The assembly's functions were then approved by the party's executive, viz. responsibility for Welsh Office expenditure and nominated bodies, together with powers in economic, industrial and planning matters.[28] It was no surprise when the Wales Trade Union Council at its conference decided to support the proposals.[29] Neil Kinnock, although he supported the proposals, admitted that they would not be given priority by an incoming Labour government. Labour rejected a call for a referendum because it was agreed that it would be a manifesto commitment.[30] Interestingly, although it had been a manifesto commitment in 1974, a referendum followed in 1979 after Labour MPs including Neil Kinnock had demanded that one be held. Again, when Opposition spokesmen said that Labour's proposals would be implemented in a Labour government's first term, Neil Kinnock in an interview after the proposals had been accepted by the Labour Party in Wales's annual conference in May 1990, was again not so specific, saying that it was 'possible, – but unlikely' that the proposals would have to wait until a second term.[31] The Conservative response, as expected, was no change. Welsh Office minister, Wyn Roberts, thought that the referendum result of 1979 should be accepted and that the matter should not be revisited, and his fellow minister, Nicholas Bennett, criticized the proposals because the assembly unlike local authorities would not have revenue raising powers.[32] Margaret Thatcher later in the year was adamant that no changes in the machinery of government were necessary. Robin Reeves quotes her response when questioned, 'The present constitutional relationships continue to serve us well'.[33] There was a mixed response from other opposition parties. Dafydd Wigley (Plaid Cymru, Caernarfon) deemed them a 'pathetic flop', but the Liberal Democrats at their annual conference in September supported a raft of constitutional changes, including an assembly for Wales.[34]

Opinion was also divided within the press, both local and national. The *South Wales Argus*, published in Newport, declared in its editorial that the recommendations fell short of what was expected and what was proposed for Scotland. There should be parity between Wales and Scotland. Also, the issue was given insufficient priority by Labour. The paper claimed that the party appeared 'coy about treating Wales as a nation with its own language and culture'.[35] The *Western Mail* thought that the Labour Party was to be commended because it had 'pushed the boat out on decentralised government for Wales'. It considered the dismissal of devolution without reservation by the secretary of state David Hunt, who represented Wirral West, 'insulting'.[36] Later in October *The Times*, in its assessment of the political situation in Wales, thought that a demand for a degree of autonomy should be recognized. It stated:

Governments have regularly bought off the Welsh by loading them with infrastructure projects and regional grants – they are entitled to a more dignified form of rule than that of colonial administrators from London.

They should have greater self-government, with a measure of ministerial accountability to a locally elected assembly in Cardiff.[37]

There was still a degree of uncertainty as to when Labour would introduce legislation establishing an assembly, if it formed the next government. In November 1990, Peter Hain, the prospective Labour candidate in the Neath by-election, joined the debate demanding that an assembly be given priority by an incoming Labour government.[38] This intervention was quite significant because after his election as member of parliament in April 1991, he was to campaign diligently for an assembly during the next six years.

Decisions taken on the machinery of government could affect local authorities, and so when Labour made a firm commitment to establish an assembly, the counties made their views known. The Assembly of Welsh Counties supported a regional council that would be responsible for Welsh Office functions and those of nominated bodies, and would not impinge on the responsibilities of local authorities. It also supported the reorganization of local authorities on a unitary basis.[39] Opposition from local authorities had contributed to the defeat of Labour's proposals in the 1970s.

Meanwhile, it seemed that the Conservative Party's opposition to an assembly was becoming less solid. David Hunt maintained that he had not reached a 'final decision' on the demand for an assembly, because there were 'uncertainties and ambiguities about the respective responsibilities of the Secretary of State and of the

Assembly and about the powers of the Assembly'. He was not convinced that there would not be conflict between an assembly and the Welsh Office over responsibilities and finance.[40] Wyn Roberts declared that the government would be prepared to consider ideas for an assembly as 'the apex of local government' which he emphasized 'would not involve a conflict between the role of the Welsh Office and the role of a national body', but the issue had to be approached with 'an open mind'.[41] The Conservative government was adamant that the role of the Welsh Office, its power base, had to be safeguarded. This may have prompted the Assembly of Welsh Counties to rethink its approach and to propose a council that would only be responsible for the work of nominated bodies. Therefore, there would not be a conflict of interest with the Welsh Office. The council envisaged would initially be indirectly elected, comprising of all MPs from Welsh constituencies together with a similar number of local authority representatives, but it could eventually become directly elected.[42] Later in October, for some unknown reason, the Assembly of Welsh Counties was to propose another option, viz. an assembly to 'oversee local government in Wales'.[43]

A general election was not imminent, but Labour confirmed in a draft of its manifesto, *Better Way for the 1990s*, that a Scottish parliament would be created and an assembly for Wales and regional administrations in England would follow.[44] Barry Jones (Alyn and Deeside), Opposition spokesman on Welsh affairs, added that the assembly in Wales would administer certain Welsh Office functions and those of nominated bodies.[45] Labour had maintained that proposals for Wales and the English regions would be implemented concurrently, but later in the year Bryan Gould, Opposition spokesman on the environment, would indicate that devolution to Scotland and Wales would precede devolution to England, 'because the English regions do not have the infrastructure of government that the Welsh and Scottish Offices provide'.[46] That would seem the natural way to proceed, bearing in mind also that support for regional assemblies in England was not guaranteed. David Hunt, however, now dismissed the whole idea of an assembly and announced that he planned to establish an economic forum, an idea floated first by the Association of Welsh Districts. It would comprise of local authority representatives, together with trade union and business leaders to advise on economic issues.[47] Hunt, speaking at the party's Welsh conference, described the proposal to create an assembly as a 'nightmare' and claimed that it would be run by 'socialist machine politicians'.[48] Those comments did not enhance the debate.

After the 1979 fiasco, Labour had always resisted a demand for a referendum on the party's proposals and that

was still the policy, but Neil Kinnock was not so definite
when he said that an assembly would only be introduced
'with consent'.[49] The Conservative MP for Cardiff North,
Gwilym Jones, called for a referendum and Alan Williams,
now a backbencher, followed suit. He said that, because
an assembly had been rejected by a huge majority in the
1979 referendum, it could only be established after it had
been approved in a referendum.[50] Jonathan Evans too
persisted in his demand for a referendum.[51] The *Western
Mail* did not support a referendum since it 'would only
create an emotive atmosphere, fraught with political
scare tactics –'.[52] Keith Raffan (Conservative, Delyn) who
had decided to leave the House of Commons at the end
of the parliament and who had supported devolution for
some time, wanted a statement that the Conservative
Party would 'seek all political views on devolution and a
referendum' inserted in its election manifesto.[53]

Interestingly, John Major unlike Margaret Thatcher
whom he had succeeded as prime minister, did not rule
out a debate on devolution, thinking that if the issue
was widely discussed then it would be abandoned.[54] The
Western Mail was solid in its demand that an assembly be
established, but argued that Labour's proposals needed
to be more robust.[55] Government ministers, other than
Welsh Office ministers, joined in the debate. Environment
minister, David Trippier, argued that the role of Welsh MPs

would change with powers devolved to an assembly and ceded to Brussels.[56] John Patten, minister of state, Home Office, claimed that the nature of Labour's proposals was determined by the strength of the opposition. Hence, the promise of a parliament in Scotland where the Scottish National Party was a real threat, but only assemblies in Wales and the regions of England where there was less of a threat to Labour electorally.[57]

In the period prior to the general election in 1992, the question of when Labour, if successful, would implement its proposals was raised again. Anita Gale, the Labour Party in Wales's organizer, stated that the reorganization of local government and the creation of unitary authorities would precede the creation of an assembly.[58] Meanwhile, Barry Jones declared that an assembly could be established early in the parliament, if Labour was victorious.[59] However, Neil Kinnock only pledged that an assembly would be established during the lifetime of the parliament, if Labour won the election.[60] If the reform of government in Wales and the English regions was to proceed at the same time, as indicated by Bryan Gould in a BBC interview, then legislation would probably not be introduced early in the parliament.[61] Gould's view regarding the timing of the legislation was contrary to the one he had expressed four months earlier. He also conceded that the first election to an assembly might not take place before a second Labour term. Scotland was a greater priority, as John Maxton (Labour, Glasgow Cathcart) declared, 'In Scotland we have the ability to start a process of decentralisation. It will act as a catalyst for the rest of the United Kingdom.'[62] The Labour general election manifesto promised a Scottish parliament with tax raising powers and was to be established in the first year.[63] In Wales, Labour's manifesto stated, 'We will establish an elected Welsh assembly in Cardiff with powers and functions which reflect the existing administrative structure.'[64] That imprecise statement implied that the party was unsure as to which specific functions should be devolved. Barry Jones who had previously said that an assembly would be established early in the next parliament now shared Neil Kinnock's view, saying that one would be established during the next parliament.[65]

The Conservative position remained unchanged. The priority was 'a Welsh Economic Council to bring together the various bodies with interests in inward investment, tourism and small business to advise the Secretary of State'.[66] *The Times* condemned John Major's steadfast refusal to consider any form of devolution, saying it would be 'more likely to precipitate a break-up of the Union than fulfilment of the demands of the Welsh and the Scots to have more say in their own affairs'.[67] Conservatives of course had always stressed that their party was the one that would maintain the Union. Indeed, the party's title is Conservative and Unionist Party. The *Western Mail* in a leading article said that a speech by John Major on devolution was 'scaremongering on a hysterical scale', and accused him of 'defending the vested interests of the South-East of England'.[68] David Hunt was concerned that any changes introduced would jeopardize the secretary of state's position in the cabinet, and Ian Grist, Conservative parliamentary candidate, Cardiff Central, raised questions regarding the changed role of Welsh MPs if an assembly was created, viz. the West Lothian question, and that issue was also raised by *The Times*. The paper declared, 'Unless the English had their own national or regional assemblies to deal with domestic English affairs, Westminster would need to be weighted in England's favour'.[69] Keith Raffan, in his last contribution to the debate, urged electors to vote for parties that supported devolution and were likely to succeed.[70]

Labour lost a fourth successive general election to the Conservatives in April 1992 and Neil Kinnock, its leader in the last two elections, resigned. He was succeeded in July by John Smith. Following the Conservative victory and no likelihood of an assembly being established the *Western Mail*, in its leading article, suggested that the government should establish indirectly elected bodies in Scotland, Wales and the regions of England in order that people could 'participate in the processes of government'.[71] Days later it declared that in Wales, in order to make some progress, David Hunt's economic council could be 'a half-way stage to the kind of constitutional reform that is needed throughout Britain'. In the paper's view, 'it could become a useful framework for transition to a directly elected all-Wales body' which would be preferable to the status quo.[72]

Prior to the general election, the Campaign for a Welsh Assembly had inserted an advertisement in the *Western Mail* on 2 April entitled 'Let's make it happen', with 900 signatures declaring support for an assembly and a post-election constitutional conference to draft a bill for such a body. A constitutional convention could then be set up as in Scotland. The petition was not signed by any Labour parliamentary candidate, and the party issued a statement that a victory at the general election would enable it to establish an assembly in the next parliament.[73] That was not to be. Peter Hain, shortly after the election, suggested that Labour should set up an all-party convention to pressurize the government to undertake constitutional reform, and although a number of unions did not support the proposal, the creation of a convention was carried at the annual conference of the Wales Trade Union Council.[74] A convention was later supported by Jon Owen Jones (Labour, Cardiff Central), but Welsh Labour MPs rejected the idea with Alan Williams speaking out against

devolution.[75] The renewed effort in support of an assembly
had earlier provoked a response from the director of the
Confederation of British Industry in Wales. Ian Kelsall
warned that there would be 'disastrous consequences' for
industry and commerce following the establishment of an
assembly.[76] Wales Young Conservatives too responded by
launching an anti-Welsh assembly campaign in Cardiff on
27 June.[77]

John Smith, as minister of state, privy council office,
played a prominent role in the devolution debates in the
1970s, and his election as leader was to result in a change in
Labour's stance on the issue. He promised when contesting
the leadership that it would be 'very high on the agenda',
if he were successful.[78] In June, in advance of John Smith's
election as leader, the Labour Party in Wales executive had
decided to establish a commission to review its policy on
the establishment of an assembly. Later in September, it
was announced that the eight-person commission would be
chaired by K.S. Hopkins, former Mid Glamorgan director
of education. It would consider the granting of legislative
powers to an assembly, and the views of party members
were to be sought by way of a questionnaire indicating the
policy as it stood and inviting suggestions for changes.[79]

After the general election, David Hunt was reappointed
secretary of state, and he proceeded to set up a Welsh
Economic Council. John Osmond quotes the secretary

of state's aim, viz. to bring together 'the key business and economic interest groups to discuss how best to co-ordinate support and accelerate progress'.[80] Significantly, in December 1992, Ron Davies (Labour, Caerphilly) now Opposition spokesman on Welsh affairs, joined in the debate. He was to play a central role during the next five years. Davies was strongly in favour of a democratic assembly and thought that such an institution, as quoted in Osmond's article, was 'needed for the sake of industry, jobs and regeneration', an assertion he was to repeat several times in the coming years.[81] Davies, leading Labour's assault on the government's proposals for the reform of local government, said that the party would not co-operate over David Hunt's Local Government Reform Bill unless there was provision in it for an assembly. Interestingly, Neil Kinnock, now a backbencher, launched an attack on the government's White Paper and also demanded 'a strategic democratically-elected body for Wales' that could supervise legislation and take executive decisions.[82] The Labour Party in Wales executive urged all Labour MPs 'to oppose vigorously' the government's White Paper because of the omission of a Welsh assembly.[83] When John Major reshuffled his government in May 1993, David Hunt was replaced by John Redwood, the member for Wokingham, as secretary of state. This appointment of a person to the far right of the Conservative Party was greeted with a 'storm of protest' when he took office on 27 May.[84]

The Campaign for a Welsh Assembly was still active and decided to change its name to the Parliament for Wales Campaign, and to launch a petition requesting that a parliament be created.[85] The petition was launched at the National Eisteddfod at Builth Wells in 1993, and representatives of all political parties except the Conservatives agreed to sign it simultaneously. Ron Davies signed for Labour.[86] Early in the following year the Parliament for Wales Campaign organized a conference, but as in 1950 the Labour Party in Wales instructed its MPs not to attend such a meeting. Peter Hain and Jon Owen Jones defied the order.[87]

In the space of two years the Labour Party faced a leadership election due to the sudden death of John Smith in May 1994. One of the contenders, Tony Blair, who had supported a Welsh assembly at the Labour Party conference in 1993 was still a firm supporter, nevertheless emphasized that it would be for the party to decide when and how to proceed.[88] During his leadership campaign, he said that there had been a huge increase in the influence exerted by quangos (quasi autonomous non governmental organizations) and they had usurped many local authority powers.[89] His campaign was successful and he assumed the leadership of the party in July 1994. In the Fabian Society pamphlet *Socialism* he described quangos as 'among the worst features of our centralising tendency of government', and in an interview confirmed that legislation for devolved government in Scotland and Wales would be a priority in the first year of a Labour government.[90]

Ron Davies believed that the mood in Wales was in favour of an assembly with both executive and legislative functions.[91] Both he and former secretary of state for Wales Cledwyn Hughes (now Lord Cledwyn) were members of the Labour Party in Wales's policy commission, chaired by K.S. Hopkins, which had decided to undertake a public consultation exercise in different locations to hear the views of organizations supporting the devolution of government.[92] Whether many people were convinced of the need for an assembly, let alone one with both executive and legislative roles, was debatable. Tony Blair wanted 'genuine political and democratic devolution', but Ian Lang, secretary of state for Scotland, said Blair's devolution agenda was a 'failure of judgement of massive proportions – a recipe for constitutional chaos and Government paralysis'.[93] Labour had linked the granting of a Scottish parliament and a Welsh assembly with regional assemblies in England, but Tony Blair recognized that developments in England would 'depend on the support being there...'[94] There was, he admitted in an interview with Tom Condon, no consensus about regional assemblies in England, and therefore a commitment could not be made, he said, until it was 'clear that the support and pressure for that is there'.[95]

Tony Blair was aware that there was dissent among Welsh Labour MPs. Llew Smith (Blaenau Gwent) had demanded a referendum in December 1994 to decide whether an assembly should be established and he repeated it the following January.[96] At the Labour Party in Wales annual conference, Blair made it quite clear that he expected MPs 'to be serious and disciplined in promoting' the party's policy on devolution.[97] His advice was not heeded because Ray Powell (Ogmore), like Llew Smith, was to call for a referendum.[98] The case for public bodies to be democratically elected was strengthened when the Nolan Committee in its report on standards in public life stated, 'There is much concern about appointments to quango boards and a widespread belief that these are not always made on merit'.[99]

The Labour Party in Wales policy commission had advocated that the manner of election to an assembly should be the traditional first-past-the post method. This was accepted by the party's executive in Wales.[100] Ron Davies, however, was of the opinion that the assembly should be elected by a method of proportional representation to enable it to win the support of the majority of the electorate.[101] He realized that support for an assembly had to be forthcoming from members of other parties and from those who had no allegiance to any party. He also realized that the support of local government leaders was a necessity and confirmed that no local government functions would be transferred to an assembly.[102] In short, different interests had to be accommodated.

Plaid Cymru president, Dafydd Wigley, was not immediately forthcoming in his support for Labour's proposals as they stood. He stated that the proposals would have to be strengthened if Labour did not have an overall majority in the next parliament and relied on his party's support. But the *Western Mail* in its leading article thought that Wigley was 'enough of a pragmatist to accept Labour's half-a-loaf rather than no loaf at all'. Nevertheless, the paper thought that Labour's proposals were 'ill-considered and unsatisfactory'.[103] It was to repeat its standpoint later when it referred to Labour's proposals as 'ill-thought out', and urged the party to adopt a method of proportional representation to ensure that the whole of Wales was represented in an assembly. Doing so would gain the support of minor parties, Plaid Cymru and the Liberal Democrats, and would thwart Conservative attempts to abolish the assembly later.[104] Under a future Conservative government the abolition of an assembly could perhaps be a possibility, bearing in mind that Margaret Thatcher had abolished the Greater London Council ten years earlier in 1986. The *Western Mail* noted later in the year, that a statement by John Major suggested that such a fate would not befall a Welsh assembly.[105] Ron Davies again argued that proportional representation as a method of election was a way of making the assembly more inclusive, but apparently Tony Blair was not in favour.[106] Such a method of election, of course, would reduce Labour's chances of dominating an elected body.

The *Western Mail* in a leading article again admitted that it was 'highly sceptical' regarding Labour's policy, but made the point that the decision taken in the referendum of 1979 had 'virtually no relevance'.[107] That was a blow to the Conservatives's case that the result should stand. Confirmation came from Tony Blair's office that an assembly would be permitted to pass secondary legislation, that is, legislation that parliament had delegated to the secretary of state.[108] Ron Davies confirmed that the Welsh Office's £7 billion budget and the responsibilities of nominated bodies would be administered by the assembly.[109] In his view the success of a Welsh assembly would be judged on whether or not there was an improvement economically and socially in the country.[110] Earlier the *Western Mail* had expressed the same view.[111] However, the assembly's revenue would be allocated by the United Kingdom Treasury and the levers of power would remain in Whitehall, so the assembly's role in economic matters would be a limited one. The *South Wales Echo* was critical of Labour's proposals. It called for the strengthening of Labour's policy so that it had 'teeth to effect real change in Wales'. Like Scotland, it should be granted legislative and tax raising powers. In its view, if an assembly was not granted such powers, then Wales would be 'best served by solid and continued representation in Westminster'.[112] In contrast, Ron Davies in an article in the *Western Mail* claimed that the assembly would enable efforts to be refocused on a 'more effective strategy for economic development'.[113]

A report on the implementation of constitutional reform in Wales raised the issue of a referendum prior to legislation. Labour's proposals were to be a manifesto commitment and therefore a referendum was deemed unnecessary.[114] Within days, Labour had reversed its decision and decided to hold a referendum. The *Western Mail* welcomed the change, and *The Guardian* reported that a pre-legislative referendum would make it more difficult for the Conservatives to make it an issue in the general election.[115] The *Western Mail* also assured voters that a referendum would enable them to vote Labour at a general election, without actually supporting an assembly at the same time.[116]

In *New Labour New Life for Britain* Labour's position was quite clear. It maintained that there was a desire for a measure of devolution and the need to extend democracy in Wales. Whether that was the case was questionable. Legislation would be introduced in the first year of a Labour government, and the assembly would take over Welsh Office functions and its powers to legislate on secondary issues and would 'reform and democratise the quango state'. The pamphlet stated, 'The aim is to strengthen our system of government and reject narrow nationalism'. A White Paper setting out the proposals would precede a referendum, and a 'Yes' vote would enable legislation to proceed quickly through its parliamentary stages.[117] William Hague, the member for Richmond in Yorkshire who had been appointed secretary of state welcomed a referendum, but thought it should not be held prior to legislation being passed in parliament. He was to repeat that view when The Referendums (Scotland and Wales) Bill was being debated in parliament.[118] *Cytûn* (Churches Together in Wales) in a report, *Wales: A Moral Society?*, was in agreement with Labour's proposals. The group that produced the report was chaired by the right reverend Rowan Williams, bishop of Monmouth, later to be appointed archbishop of Wales and then archbishop of Canterbury. An assembly was supported as were unitary authorities and the proliferation of quangos was disapproved.[119] The previous August, the archbishop of Wales, the right reverend Alwyn Rice Jones, had added his support for a 'measure of independence and experience of self-government'.[120]

The Labour Party in Wales's executive which had unanimously agreed that a referendum was necessary, decided to reconvene its policy commission to reconsider the method of election to an assembly. This was Tony Blair's wish and he wanted to meet the executive to discuss the matter.[121] Blair was originally against a method of proportional representation, but he had a change of mind. He had probably come to the conclusion that the traditional first-past-the-post method would not garner sufficient cross-party support for a 'Yes' campaign in a referendum and deliver an assembly. This change led to opposition from Labour MPs. Llew Smith had always opposed an assembly and his constituency party too were to support him.[122] A method of proportional representation was unacceptable to Allan Rogers (Rhondda) and Denzil Davies. They were later joined by Ted Rowlands and Ray Powell.[123] The Labour Party in Wales's executive, in line with Tony Blair's wishes, endorsed a method of proportional representation and its conference later approved the decision.[124] In an assembly of 60 members, 40 members would be elected by the traditional first-past-the-post method and 20 members by a method of proportional representation, thus ensuring that the assembly would not be the domain of Labour members.[125]

A referendum would only result if Labour was successful in the general election, yet William Hague began to address the outcome of a 'Yes' vote in a referendum prior to the election. Hague stated that if there was a 'Yes' vote 'we would be stuck with things for the foreseeable future'.[126] He shared John Major's view that a 'Yes' vote would be irreversible.[127] That statement could tip the balance in favour of a 'No' vote in a referendum. The Labour Party in Wales was given an assurance by Tony Blair of his support during a referendum campaign. He declared that he not only believed in devolution, but he would campaign for it in a referendum, and he reiterated his support at the Labour Party in Wales conference saying, 'I will be with you, here in Wales, campaigning for a yes vote'.[128] He certainly kept his word.

Labour's policy on devolution was gaining support. Welsh businessmen launched a business forum on devolution so that the issue could be debated freely and openly. They stressed that devolution would remedy some of the weaknesses in the existing system of government and that they would be supporting Labour's proposals.[129] Labour's proposals were also supported by Alex Carlile, leader of the Liberal Democrats in Wales, and by trade union leaders George Wright and Derek Gregory (now of Unison). Critically, Harry Jones, leader of Newport County Borough Council and the Welsh Local Government

Association, supported them.[130] The *Western Mail* which had been critical of Labour's policy now argued that not only would an assembly be a more democratic form of government, but it should also result in economic benefits, 'The right type of Assembly, which makes Wales fitter, stronger and prepared for the challenges of the 21st century, will be worth the nation's support'.[131] *The Guardian* maintained that the proposed assembly should have the same powers as the Scottish parliament. The paper stated, 'The political danger of this economy-class option is that Welsh opinion will turn against what is on offer'.[132]

Labour's manifesto for the general election stated that an assembly would be responsible for Welsh Office functions and would be able to pass secondary legislation. A referendum would be decided by a simple majority.[133] The party's dissident MPs would be expected to support the proposals in parliament, but they would be permitted to move amendments. They would also be expected to campaign for the proposals in a referendum.[134] Tony Blair's election victory on 1 May, Labour Day, saw the Conservatives suffer a crushing defeat, particularly in Wales where they held no seats. Thus, it would be difficult for them to amend the bill when legislation was brought before parliament. The result United Kingdom wide was as follows: Labour 418, Conservatives 165, Liberal Democrats 46, others 30, including Sinn Féin 2 (their MPs would not take their seats in the House of Commons). Labour majority 179.[135] Of the 40 seats in Wales, 34 were won by Labour, 4 by Plaid Cymru and 2 by the Liberal Democrats.[136] Ron Davies was appointed secretary of state and he was joined in the Welsh Office by Peter Hain and Win Griffiths (Bridgend). Tony Blair had been elected leader of the Labour Party in July 1994, and in just under three years had made Labour credible and consequently electable, but few were prepared for a landslide Labour victory. Following such a heavy defeat, John Major resigned as leader of the Conservative Party almost immediately on 2 May.

On 15 May, just a fortnight after the general election, the bill entitled Referendums (Scotland and Wales) was presented in the House of Commons. Initially, Tony Blair was prepared to take a hard line against dissident MPs. He declared that MPs and Labour Party members could be disciplined and even expelled if they openly campaigned against devolution for Scotland and Wales.[137] Peter Hain appealed to the anti-Tory vote. He urged people not to support the Conservatives by voting against the proposals or by not voting at all.[138] He was obviously appealing to the core Labour vote, particularly in the populous areas of south Wales. Alan Williams who had continually opposed measures of devolution quite naturally voiced his objections. He argued that a pre-legislative referendum would mean that people would not know what they were voting for or against.[139] He also claimed that the referendum in Scotland a week earlier would influence the vote in Wales. Speaking in the House of Commons, he said, 'If a case for devolution stands, let it stand without stage management. Give it a chance to stand or fall on its merits.'[140]

The government had facilitated a 'Yes' vote by not introducing legislation prior to the referendum which would have allowed MPs to delay the proposals or substantially amend them. It was only too apparent that the Scottish proposals would be approved in the referendum and that result would be a positive influence on the Welsh vote. As promised, MPs were allowed to table amendments when the legislation was brought before the House of Commons. Ted Rowlands and Denzil Davies did just that during the Committee Stage of the Referendums (Scotland and Wales) Bill.[141] Matthew d'Ancona quotes an interview in the *New Statesman* in July 1996 in which Tony Blair explained that the whole point of the referendum was 'to ease the passage of legislation, to give us a better chance of achieving our aim'.[142] A pre-legislative referendum would certainly give the government a better chance of achieving its aim. The Wales Trade Union Council gave its expected support to the government. Llew Smith and Allan Rogers feared that Welsh MPs would not be permitted to vote on English only matters and there would be a reduction in their numbers, although it was made clear that the assembly would not have legislative and tax-raising powers.[143] In a matter of weeks Labour's attitude towards those who opposed the policy changed. It may have been persuaded to do so because it could afford to do so with such a massive majority in the House of Commons. Tony Blair announced at a meeting of the parliamentary party that members who disagreed with the policy would not be expelled, and apparently they would also be permitted to campaign against an assembly in the referendum.[144]

The government published a White Paper *A Voice for Wales*. The assembly would have 60 members – 40 would be elected by the traditional first-past-the-post method and 20 by a method of proportional representation. Elections would be held every four years. The secretary of state's functions to be transferred would include economic development, health, education, agriculture, industry and training and powers to pass secondary legislation. The block grant would be retained and the Welsh Office's budget control would pass to the assembly.[145] The government announced that certain quangos in the economic field were to be reorganized prior to the establishment of an assembly, and Alan Williams, Denzil Davies, Ted Rowlands and Allan Rogers thought that an opportunity to dismantle numerous quangos had been lost.[146] Opponents still questioned the decision to hold the referenda on different dates. However, Peter Hain defended the decision because he said the Scottish and Welsh proposals were different. A decision on that basis could not be justified, but his argument that the media would have concentrated on the Scottish referendum, resulting in insufficient coverage of the debate in Wales, was a valid one.[147] On 31 July the act for referenda in Scotland and Wales on 11 and 18 September respectively was granted the Royal Assent, exactly 19 years to the day the ill-fated Wales Act 1978 was granted the assent.[148]

Support for the government's proposals came from local authorities and political parties. That local government powers would not be undertaken by an assembly helped to gain the support of local authority leaders. Harry Jones came out strongly in favour of the proposals yet again, claiming that an assembly would reverse the damage inflicted during the 18-year period of Conservative rule.[149] The Welsh Local Government Association was also firmly in support of the proposals. It declared that the 18-year period of Conservative government had resulted in a succession of secretaries of state unreceptive to the needs of local authorities, and in an increase in the number of nominated bodies.[150] Some nominated bodies were probably performing functions which local authorities could perform. Plaid Cymru, the Liberal Democrats and the Green Party agreed to support the government's proposals.[151]

Non-political organizations made their views known. Catholics Say 'Yes' for Wales urged all communicants to support the government. Elizabeth Haywood, director of the Confederation of British Industry in Wales, described the organization's response as 'judicious neutrality – because the argument so far has been about bridging the economic deficit rather than added economic value'.[152] Cross-party campaigns were also launched in support of and against an assembly. The Teachers Say 'Yes' for Wales campaign was launched and a Just Say 'No' campaign with George Thomas (now Viscount Tonypandy) as its president.[153] The *Western Mail* pointed out that the 'No' campaign failed to offer an alternative policy and was 'negative in more than name'.[154] A month before the referendum an opinion poll was conducted by Beaufort Research. Between 13 and 16 August, 1,003 adults at 60 locations throughout Wales were interviewed. The result was 42 per cent in favour, 22 per cent against and 36 per cent unsure or don't know.[155] The unsure or don't know percentage was a sizeable proportion of the electorate and revealed that the result could go either way.

The Labour government's campaign in Wales was a high profile one that included visits by several ministers. Cabinet ministers David Blunkett, Gordon Brown, Harriet Harman,

John Prescott, Chris Smith, Gavin Strang and significantly Donald Dewar, secretary of state for Scotland joined the campaign. While Stephen Byers and Joan Ruddock, both junior ministers, played a part. Also, on the day prior to the referendum, MPs from England and Scotland were involved in canvassing. The prime minister, Tony Blair, set an example of what was expected from ministers and visited Wales on two occasions with visits to north and south Wales. His visits were covered by the London press and this helped to give the Welsh campaign a higher profile. This was a plus for Labour's campaign because many people in Wales read London newspapers rather than regional ones. The Conservative campaign was led by its newly-elected leader William Hague and Michael Ancram, the member for Devizes and the party's spokesman on constitutional affairs, and the absence of former ministers was only too apparent. Labour concentrated on the populous areas of south-east and north-east Wales with ministerial visits to Cardiff, Llantrisant, Merthyr Tydfil, Newport, Wrexham and Deeside. The Conservatives too targeted Cardiff, Newport and Wrexham and also sought support outside the industrial areas with visits to Caernarfon, Llandrindod Wells and Monmouth.[156]

The government's campaign received a boost when Rhondda and Swansea West constituency Labour parties announced in the week preceding the referendum that they did not support their MPs, Allan Rogers and Alan Williams, who intended with Ray Powell and Llew Smith to vote 'No'.[157] Michael Foot, Llew Smith's predecessor as MP for Blaenau Gwent did not share the MP's view and said that neither did the constituency party.[158] There was further encouragement when Ian Spratling, chairman of the Confederation of British Industry in Wales, criticized the Just Say 'No' campaign for sending out the 'wrong signals'. The campaign's dire warnings, without foundation, that unemployment and business closures would result were sure to frighten off investors.[159]

The Scottish result was an overwhelming endorsement of the government's policy – 1,775,045 (74.29 per cent) were for a Scottish parliament and 1,512,889 (63.48 per cent) were for tax varying powers. There was a 60.16 per cent turnout.[160] Commenting on that vote the Western Mail in its leading article said, 'The principal impact of Scotland's decision is that it has released the genie of constitutional change from the bottle'.[161] Following that result, Wyn Roberts, now a life peer, said that if there was a 'Yes' vote in Wales the proposals should be strengthened and a cabinet-type system introduced as in Scotland.[162] This was later accepted by the government. Ted Rowlands declared that he would support the government's proposals because he supported the principle of devolution, although in his view some aspects were 'seriously flawed'.[163] Ray

Powell had earlier pledged to campaign for a 'No' vote, but Allan Rogers apparently did not participate in any campaigning.[164]

In the days prior to the referendum the government received further support. Graham Banfield, director of the Wales Council for Voluntary Action, came out in favour of the proposals and the Farmers' Union of Wales did likewise.[165] The union was formed in 1955 when farmers from Cardiganshire and Carmarthenshire decided to break away from the National Farmers' Union. The right reverend B.N.Y. Vaughan, former bishop of Swansea and Brecon, in a letter to the *Western Mail* on polling day, urged voters to 'Cast off the Welsh NOT which has hung around the neck of past generations and say Yes'. The newspaper in its leading article on the same day maintained that 'in virtually every important measure Wales has been badly governed for far too long'. Labour's proposed assembly, despite its limitations, in the paper's view offered the best chance of effecting an improvement. The article ended, 'It is time to say Yes for Wales'.[166] In sharp contrast the heading of *The Daily Telegraph*'s editorial comment was quite explicit too, 'Just say Na', translated a straight 'No'.[167] Tony Blair's message to Welsh voters was that it was 'make or break time for Wales, a historic turning point'. He warned that they would not 'get another chance – opportunities like this only come round in a generation'. William Hague could only say that the economy would be damaged and that tensions would arise between the various nations of the United Kingdom.[168]

Despite the fact that a bilingual summary of the government's proposals entitled *A Voice for Wales/Llais i Gymru* had been sent to every household, and the high profile campaign waged by Labour immediately following a landslide victory in the general election, the result was extremely close. In fact, the proposals were accepted with a wafer-thin majority: 559,419 (50.3 per cent) supported the government's proposals, while 552,698 (49.7 per cent) voted 'No' in a low turnout of just 50.12 per cent.[169] The highest turnout was in Gwynedd (59.8 per cent) and the lowest in Flintshire (41.1 per cent). The biggest majority in favour was 33.1 per cent in Neath Port Talbot and against in Monmouthshire (35.8 per cent). The smallest majority for was on the Isle of Anglesey (1.8 per cent) and against in Torfaen (0.3 per cent). There were 'Yes' votes in local authority areas represented by dissident MPs, viz. Bridgend, Rhondda Cynon Taff, Swansea, Blaenau Gwent and Carmarthenshire. Local authority areas represented by Welsh Office ministers also registered 'Yes' votes, viz. Caerphilly, Neath Port Talbot and Bridgend. Some areas were represented by more than one MP holding divergent views. Wrexham and Flintshire, the populous areas in north Wales, and

Cardiff and Newport in south Wales voted 'No'.[170] The vote in Newport was a disappointment for the government, particularly since the County Borough Council's newspaper *Newport Matters* was sent to every household, and in its September issue the four-paged colourful tabloid-sized publication was devoted entirely to the merits of an assembly. Harry Jones's message to electors in the paper was, 'The creation of an Assembly will put the important decisions affecting all our lives back into our own hands', but the majority was obviously not convinced.[171] Speaking in 1995, Lord Cledwyn had said, 'it is our duty to strive to ensure that we have an elected assembly to herald the dawn of the new century –'. It did come about, but only just.[172] The *Western Mail* in a post-referendum leading article admitted that the road that lay ahead for the nation was unclear and added, 'But that is preferable to the constitutional stagnation which threatened to leave it lagging behind in Britain and Europe'.[173] Whether the people of Wales made the right decision can only be determined after a period of time. Ron Davies, in an address to Cardiff Business Club in November 1996, had reiterated the viewpoint that the assembly would be assessed on its ability to strengthen the economy and raise the standard of living in Wales.[174]

The reversal of the 1979 referendum result was due

to a combination of factors. The Labour Party in Wales was reluctant to support a Welsh assembly so soon after the calamitous referendum in 1979. Moves for greater autonomy for Scotland and the English regions helped to change attitudes, coupled with the policies of the Thatcher governments, particularly those that resulted in heavy job losses in the coal and steel industries, although whether having an assembly would have made a significant difference is doubtful. The Labour Party made an increase in nominated bodies, often chaired by Conservative Party members or sympathizers, an issue, and this was supported by local authorities who felt that their powers were being eroded. They were won over too because the final proposals did not include the loss of any local government functions and did not include proposals for local government reorganization. The Campaign for a Welsh Assembly, later the Parliament for Wales Campaign played a part in keeping devolution to the fore in Welsh politics, and as a cross-party organization attracted the support of people who otherwise may not have become involved in the debate. Opposition from Welsh Labour MPs sabotaged Labour's plans in the 1970s and there was opposition to the Blair government's proposals, but it was more restrained and did not have the impact such opposition had in the 1970s. The government's huge majority may have deterred those MPs who had reservations regarding the policy from withholding their support.

Labour, unlike the Conservatives, pursued a vigorous campaign in which ministers were prominent as well as MPs from other parts of the United Kingdom. This contrasted sharply with what could be termed a low-key Conservative campaign. It was left to William Hague and Michael Ancram to try to convince voters to reject a Labour proposal that was supported by other parties. If the Conservatives had taken the matter more seriously the result may have been different. Dafydd Wigley praised the efforts of Ron Davies, Peter Hain and Win Griffiths, and the collaborative efforts of all parties which supported an assembly. He summed up the situation when he said, 'Where there is a degree of consensus it is possible to move an agenda forward'.[175] Also, Labour had succeeded in winning over non-political organizations that thought that there was merit in the proposals, in that they would have a positive effect on the lives of Welsh men and women.

Critical though was the influence of the Labour leader and prime minister, Tony Blair. Blair prior to John Smith's death had supported devolution and after his election as leader had maintained Labour's commitment to it. He masterminded the whole approach to the subject and everything worked as planned. Blair realized that in Wales the subject was certainly of interest to a minority active in political circles, but perhaps less so to the population as a whole. To win the support of people of different political persuasions, he insisted, after initial doubts, that there should be an element of proportional representation that would ensure that other parties would be represented in the assembly, thereby making the proposals appeal to their members. Holding a pre-legislative referendum and securing a 'Yes' vote enabled the government to implement its proposals. Writing later Blair emphasized that a pre-legislative referendum was devised 'so that people could take a decision on the principle first', because once it had been approved by the people it could not be overturned by the House of Lords.[176] There was not to be a repeat of the 1970s scenario, when devolution was the subject of lengthy debates in parliament before being passed, only to be rejected in a referendum. Also, the holding of the referendum in Scotland prior to the one in Wales was a masterstroke. However, at the end of the day, the majority in favour was minimal, and perhaps it is not unreasonable to think that it was Tony Blair's leadership and campaigning skills that may just have been the factors that tipped the scales in favour of a 'Yes' vote.

Anatole Kaletsky, commenting in 2001 on Tony Blair's legacy up to that point, said that his period in office would be remembered by historians 'for one and only one event:

the transformation of the British constitution'. He went on to say:

> Sweeping away the 800-year tradition of hereditary peerage and abolishing the United Kingdom as a centralised, unitary state will surely be seen, by future generations of Britons as infinitely more important than administrative tinkering with the health service, reform of the Labour Party or even the imminent decision on the euro.

Kaletsky added, 'Mr Blair's constitutional reforms deserve good marks' and he awarded him 8 out of 10.[177] Noreen Burrows agrees that devolution was 'part of the process of modernisation of the United Kingdom constitution', but points out that it was also 'part of a New Labour agenda…'[178]

Contrary to what he had claimed previously, Tony Blair writing about his time as prime minister said that he was 'never a passionate devolutionist', but thought that it was 'inevitable'. In a changing world, with nation states yielding powers to multinational institutions, 'there would be inexorable pressure to devolve power downwards to where people felt greater connection'. Blair and New Labour realized that this would be the case in the United Kingdom, and that more pressure would come from Scotland than from other parts and he did not want people there to think that 'the choice was status quo or separatism'.[179] Scotland then was a priority, more so than Wales and the English regions.

References

1   *Western Mail*, 12 January 1983.
2   *Ibid.*, 24 January 1983.
3   *Ibid.*, 10 March 1983.
4   *Ibid.*, 9 October 1985.
5   *Ibid.*, 18 March 1986.
6   *Ibid.*, 1 May 1986.
7   *The Daily Express*, 26 August 1986.
8   *Ibid.*, 26 August 1986.
9   *Western Mail*, 18 March 1986, 20 May 1987.
10   *Ibid.*, 13 June 1987.
11   *Ibid.*, 18 July 1987.
12   *Ibid.*, 21 May 1988.
13   *Ibid.*, 23 May 1988.
14   *Ibid.*, 1 July 1988.
15   *Ibid.*, 7 September 1988.
16   *The Guardian*, 28 November 1988.
17   *Western Mail*, 9 January 1989.
18   *Ibid.*, 21 January 1989.
19   *Ibid.*, 30 January, 1 February 1989.
20   *South Wales Argus*, 27 January 1989.
21   *Western Mail*, 28 January 1989.
22   *Ibid.*, 17 February 1989.

23   *Ibid.*, 10 May 1989.

24   *Ibid.*, 15 May 1989.

25   *Ibid.*, 15 December 1989.

26   *Ibid.*, 14 February 1990.

27   *Ibid.*, 23 January 1990.

28   *Ibid.*, 16 April 1990.

29   *Ibid.*, 4 May 1990.

30   *Ibid.*, 20 April 1990.

31   *Western Mail*, 21 May 1990; *South Wales Echo*, 19 June 1990.

32   *Western Mail*, 28, 20 April 1990.

33   *Ibid.*, 19 September 1990.

34   *Ibid.*, 20 April, 19 September 1990.

35   *South Wales Argus*, 20 April 1990.

36   *Western Mail*, 20 April, 10 July 1990.

37   *The Times*, 27 October 1990.

38   *Western Mail*, 14 November 1990.

39   *Ibid.*, 15 January, 26 February 1991.

40   *Ibid.*, 28 March, 4 April 1991.

41   *Ibid.*, 30 March 1991.

42   *Ibid.*, 8 May 1991.

43   *Ibid.*, 3 October 1991.

44   *Ibid.*, 7 April 1991.

45   *Ibid.*, 19 April 1991.

46   *Ibid.*, 1 November 1991.

47   *Ibid.*, 8 May, 17 June, 25 July 1991, 16 April 1992.

48   *Wales on Sunday*, 16 June 1991.

49   *Western Mail*, 2, 4 October 1991.

50   *Ibid.*, 18 October, 19 November 1991.

51   *Ibid.*, 3 February 1992.

52   *Ibid.*, 3 February 1992.

53   *Ibid.*, 10 February 1992.

54   *Ibid.*, 5 February 1992.

55   *Ibid.*, 2 January 1992.

56   *Mail on Sunday*, 5 January 1992.

57   *The Guardian*, 21 January 1992.

58   *Western Mail*, 11 February 1992.

59   *Ibid.*, 26 February 1992.

60   *Ibid.*, 29 February 1992.

61   *Ibid.*, 2 March 1992.

62   *Ibid.*, 6 March 1992.

63   *The Daily Telegraph*, 13 March 1992.

64   *The Times*, 19 March 1992.

65   *Western Mail*, 19 March 1992.

66   *The Times*, 19 March 1992.

67   *Ibid.*, 20 March 1992.

68   *Western Mail*, 30 March 1992.

69   *The Times*, 20, 28 March, 7 April 1992.

70   *Western Mail*, 8 April 1992.

71   *Ibid.*, 11 April 1992.

72   *Ibid.*, 13 April 1992.

73   *Ibid.*, 2 April 1992.

74   *Ibid.*, 20 April, 1 May 1992.

75   *Ibid.*, 10 June 1992.

76   *Ibid.*, 22 May 1992.

77   *Ibid.*, 26 June 1992.

78   *Ibid.*, 3 June 1992.

79   *Ibid.*, 23 June, 30 September, 28 October 1992.

80   *Ibid.*, 28 December 1992.

81   *Ibid.*, 28 December 1992.

82   *Ibid.*, 21 January, 9 March 1993.

83   *Ibid.*, 18 May 1993.

84   *Ibid.*, 28 May 1993.

85   *Ibid.*, 7 June 1993.

86   *Ibid.*, 2 August 1993.

87   *Ibid.*, 2 March 1994.

88   *Ibid.*, 24, 27 June 1994.

89   *Ibid.*, 16 July 1994.

90   *Western Mail*, 25 July 1994; *The Daily Telegraph*, 26 July 1994.

91   *Western Mail*, 29 July 1994.

92   *Ibid.*, 12 September 1994.

93   *Western Mail*, 18 November 1994; *The Daily Telegraph*, 15 October 1994.

94   *The Guardian*, 10 January 1995.

95   *Scotland on Sunday*, 5 March 1995.

96   *Western Mail*, 14 December 1994, 16 January 1995.

97   *Ibid.*, 20 May 1995.

98   *The Daily Telegraph*, 17 June 1995.

99   *Western Mail*, 12 May 1995.

100   *Ibid.*, 11 April 1995.

101   *Ibid.*, 17 June 1995.

102   *Ibid.*, 31 August 1995.

103   *Ibid.*, 17 November 1995.

104   *Ibid.*, 6 January 1996.

105   *Ibid.*, 15 June 1996.

106   *Ibid.*, 5, 9 February 1996.

107   *Ibid.*, 1 March 1996.

108   *Ibid.*, 8 March 1996.

109   *Ibid.*, 7 June 1996.

110   *Ibid.*, 13 May 1996.

111   *Ibid.*, 8 May 1996.

112   *South Wales Echo*, 25 June 1996.

113   *Western Mail*, 25 June 1996.

114   *Ibid.*, 25 June 1996.

115   *Western Mail*, 27 June 1996; *The Guardian*, 27 June 1996.

116   *Western Mail*, 29 June 1996.

117   *Ibid.*, 5 July 1996.

118   *Western Mail*, 16 July 1996; *Parl. Deb.*, vol. 294, col. 886

119   *Western Mail*, 31 July, 1 August 1996.

120   *Ibid.*, 9 August 1995.

121   *Ibid.*, 16 July 1996.

122   *Ibid.*, 5, 6 September 1996.

123   *Ibid.*, 16 July, 10 December 1996, 28 January 1997.

124   *Ibid.*, 14 January, 1 March 1997.

125   *Ibid.*, 28 January 1997.

126   *Ibid.*, 17 February 1997.

127   *Ibid.*, 15 June 1996.

128   *Ibid.*, 3 September 1996, 1 March 1997.

129   *Ibid.*, 17 January 1997.

130   *Ibid.*, 3 March 1997.

131   *Ibid.*, 1 March 1997.

132   *The Guardian*, 17 February 1997.

133   *Western Mail*, 4 April 1997.

134   *Ibid.*, 5 April 1997.

135   *The Daily Telegraph*, 3 May 1997.

136   *Western Mail*, 3 May 1997.

137   *The Daily Telegraph*, 16 May 1997.

138   *Western Mail*, 23 May 1997.

139   *Ibid.*, 23 May 1997.

140   *Western Mail*, 23 May 1997; *The Daily Telegraph*, 23 May 1997; *Parl. Deb.*, vol. 294, col. 861.

141   *Sunday Telegraph*, 1 June 1997.

142   *Ibid.*, 1 June 1997.

143   *Western Mail*, 6, 7 June 1997.

144   *Western Mail*, 30 June 1997; *The Daily Telegraph*, 30 June, 2 July 1997.

145   *Western Mail*, 23 July 1997.

146   *Ibid.*, 24, 26 July 1997.

147   *Ibid.*, 31 July 1997.

148   *Ibid.*, 1 August 1997.

149   *Ibid.*, 30 July 1997.

150   *Ibid.*, 29 August 1997.

151   *Ibid.*, 30 August 1997.

152   *Ibid.*, 18, 27 August 1997.

153   *Ibid.*, 22 July 1997.

154   *Ibid.*, 10 July 1997.

155   *Ibid.*, 30 August 1997.

156   *Western Mail*, 8–18 September 1997; *The Daily Telegraph*, 13, 17–18 September 1997.

157   *Western Mail*, 10, 11, 12 September 1997.

158   *Ibid.*, 11 September 1997.

159   *Ibid.*, 10 September 1997.

160   *Ibid.*, 13 September 1997.

161   *Ibid.*, 12 September 1997.

162   *Ibid.*, 13 September 1997.

163   *The Daily Telegraph*, 16 September 1997.

164   *Western Mail*, 31 July 1997; *The Daily Telegraph*, 19 September 1997.

165   *Western Mail*, 15, 20 September 1997.

166   *Ibid.*, 18 September 1997.

167   *The Daily Telegraph*, 18 September 1997.

168   *Western Mail*, 17 September 1997.

169   *Ibid.*, 20 September 1997.

170   *Ibid.*, 20 September 1997.

171   *Newport Matters*, September 1997.

172   Lord Cledwyn, *Wales Yesterday and Tomorrow*, National Eisteddfod of Wales, Bro Colwyn, 1995.

173   *Western Mail*, 20 September 1997.

174   *Ibid.*, 26 November 1996.

175   *Ibid.*, 20 September 1997.

176   Tony Blair, *A Journey* (London, 2000), 252.

177   *The Times*, 23 March 2001.

178   Noreen Burrows, *Devolution* (London, 2000), 1.

179   Blair, *A Journey*, 251.

PART III

The Welsh Settlement (1998)

DEVOLUTION WITHIN THE United Kingdom has been termed asymmetric because the devolved governments in Scotland, Wales and Northern Ireland have different powers and responsibilities.[1]

The proposals for Wales were embodied in the Government of Wales Act 1998. A National Assembly for Wales was to be established, comprising of 40 members representing Welsh parliamentary constituencies and 20 representing five regional constituencies (four members per constituency). The constituency representatives were to be elected by the traditional first-past-the-post method, but the regional representatives were to be elected by a form of proportional representation.[2]

The powers granted to the Assembly were those administered by the secretary of state for Wales, viz:

- agriculture and fisheries
- culture
- economic development
- education and training
- environment
- health
- highways

- housing
- industry
- local government
- social services
- sport
- tourism
- town and country planning
- transport
- water
- Welsh language

In addition, it was granted the power to pass secondary legislation in devolved areas.[3]

To enable it to fulfil its responsibilities, the Assembly was to receive a block grant from the United Kingdom Treasury. The Welsh Office had received a block grant determined by the Barnett formula to meet its devolved responsibilities and the same formula was to apply when these responsibilities were transferred to the Assembly.[4]

The Labour government referred the devolution legislation to a cabinet committee, the Cabinet Committee on devolution to Scotland, Wales, and the Regions.[5] The home secretary, Jack Straw, was a member of that committee and writing later commented that insufficient attention had been paid to the effects of devolution.[6] One aspect that was not adequately dealt with was funding, with the result that Wales was to receive an unequal share. The Barnett formula was accepted although its relevance had diminished.[7] This was the view of Joel Barnett who had devised the formula in the 1970s when chief secretary to the Treasury. In November 1997, when funding for the devolved governments was being discussed, he wrote, 'The formula I devised to a large extent took account of different levels of income per head in England, Scotland and Wales. In those days, Scotland had a lower level of income per head than the North-East... That has changed substantially. It is a matter of what is fair now.'[8] Jack Straw agreed with Joel Barnett, but members of the Cabinet Committee on devolution to Scotland, Wales, and the Regions were reluctant to address the problem. Straw attributed this to the fact that the 'Scottish Convention', comprising of representatives of the Labour Party and Liberal Democrats, the churches and other organizations had submitted an 'extensive menu for devolution' which was more or less accepted by the committee. Also, the threat from the Scottish National Party loomed large during discussions. As a result, Scotland received a more generous settlement than it was entitled to, and Wales and the English regions were not as fairly treated as they should have been.[9] An all-party convention failed to materialize in Wales. Whether such a convention would have benefited Wales when the terms of the settlement were being discussed is open to debate.

The period from 1983 to 1998 was a determining one in the political history of Wales. Devolution was in Tony Blair's view a 'historic' change.[10] That cannot be denied, but the Welsh settlement lacked parity with Scotland in terms of its responsibilities and funding. Whether that will change in time is beyond prediction, bearing in mind that effecting constitutional change is fraught with difficulties.

References

1   Matthew Leek, Chris Seer and Ooonagh Gay, *An introduction to devolution in the U.K.*, Research Paper 03/84 (Parliament and Constitutional Centre, 17 November 2003), 3.

2   *Idem.*, 23.

3   *Idem.*, 25, 8.

4   *Idem.*, 9.

5   Jack Straw, *Last Man Standing* (London, 2012), 220.

6   *Idem.*, 218.

7   *Idem.*, 222.

8   *The Daily Telegraph*, 3 November 1997.

9   Straw, *Last Man Standing*, 221.

10   Blair, *A Journey*, 124.

Appendix

U NDER THE GOVERNMENT of Wales Act 2006, the National Assembly for Wales was permitted to pass laws 'in areas where those powers have been expressly conferred', viz:

- agriculture, forestry, animals, plants and rural development
- ancient monuments and historic buildings
- culture
- economic development
- education and training
- environment
- fire and rescue services and fire safety
- food
- health and health services
- highways and transport
- housing
- local government
- National Assembly for Wales
- public administration
- social welfare

- sport and recreation
- tourism
- devolved taxes
- town and country planning
- water and flood defence
- Welsh language

National Assembly for Wales, *Governance of Wales: Who is responsible for what?* 2–3.

★

Under the Wales Act 2017, the Conferred Powers Model of 2006 was replaced in 2018 with the Reserved Powers Model. This model permits the National Assembly for Wales to pass laws in areas that are not reserved. The powers reserved to the Westminster parliament are listed under subject headings, viz:

Part 1: General Reservations

Part 2: Specific Reservations

- financial and economic matters
- home affairs
- trade and industry
- energy
- transport

- social security, child support, pensions and compensation
- professions
- employment
- health, safety and medicines
- media, culture and sport
- justice
- land and agricultural assets
- miscellaneous

National Assembly for Wales, Research Service, *Wales Act 2017*

Index

About the Author

JOHN GILBERT EVANS was born in Ystalyfera in the Swansea Valley and educated at Ystalyfera Grammar School and the University of Wales, Aberystwyth. He gained a MA degree at the University of Wales, Swansea. After a period teaching in schools, he joined the staff of Caerleon College of Education and was, prior to his retirement, head of educational studies at the University of Wales, Newport. In 1969, he was appointed a member of a study group set up by the Welsh Council of Labour to prepare evidence to the *Royal Commission on the Constitution, 1969–1973*. In 1970, he was the Labour Party parliamentary candidate in Flint West. His book, *Devolution in Wales Claims and Responses, 1937–1979* was published in 2006.